I0458012

COMBAT OF

Love

All inquiries should be addressed to:

Book Domain LLC.
543 E Louise Dr Phoenix, Az 85050

Ordering Information:

Amount Deals. Special rebates are accessible on the amount
bought by corporations, associations, and others. For points
of interest, contact the distributor at the address above.

Printed in the United States of America.

ISBN-13 Paperback   978-1-967903-97-9
         eBook   978-1-967903-96-2

Library of Congress Control Number: 2025920771

COMBAT OF

Love

CLARENCE MCCLAIN

BOOK DOMAIN LLC

Contents

In Loving memory of
Mattie McClain Robinson,
Clarence McClain Sr., Lois McClain
Dotch, and Toranita LaShe McClain

Confusion by Love

As I sit in a world that is Lost,
people inhabited, by worldly things
searching for a life they will
never find, unless they lift
their voice and pray
and call upon Jesus
Confusion by love
there is no greater love than
Jesus Christ
That can free you from
pain, stress, suffering and
give you everlasting life
Playing a fool's game with
worldly temptation
Not understanding the price
for sin is death
Jesus brings us into your
convent where there is peace and
Joy
Confusion by love
Lord help us Living in a world knowing that we
are destined to die

Hurt by Love

Last night I dreamt I had
found the perfect woman
someone who can love and be
Loved
Looks turn Heads
when people see her
they can feel the Love
still searching for ever
lasting love
walking the floor wondering where
can I find this woman
Hurt by love
Someday that special woman
will arrive
I will receive her with open
Arms
Just to look into her eyes
to see a smile Just to feel
Love
Hurt by love

Leaving You Tonite

I call you on the phone
I call your house
your mama answer the phone
saying she don't know where you
at
you are a good man
all I could say
I am not being a fool
leaving you tonite
the kid's crying in the house
food empty from the table
house not clean
I been working twelve hours
you been gone ten hours
leaving you tonite
If drug's not your problem
then men must be your trouble
staying out forgetting family
you don't want nothing in life
Leaving you tonite

Here I Am

Hey Girl you said you
Love me
Every time I call your
house
you say call me back in an
hour
All these lies confusion only
Lead to deception
Here I am love me for me
Or let me go,
Happiness is everything
that everyone needs
Running the street and the club
only lean to hurt and pain
Here I am
Love me for me
Here I am
Love me for me
or let me go

Confusion of Knowledge

As I sit in this that is lost
a world inhabited by temptation
searching for a life never to find
they reach out there and call upon Jesus
confusion by knowledge
Jesus has become forgotten in their life
the only one that can set them
on solid ground
freedom from pain, stress, suffering
everlasting life
Playing a foolish game
thinking we are happy not understanding
the price for sin is death
confusion by knowledge
Jesus helps up bring us into your covert
where there is peace and Joy

City Light, Big City

Millions of people lost in a fog
Of broken heart
I'm just the victim
can't understand why she left me I gave
her everything a woman needs
fancy clothes, money, a brand-new car
riding around town making me
feel like a fool
I'm just a victim
City Light, Big City
spoiled by love
wanting to keep her satisfied
mental and physical
willing to change my whole life
Just to please her
Now that she is gone
I can see straight
City Light, Big City
Victim of my own circumstance
City Light, Big City

Uplifting

Sweet nights Always bring
together moments to remember
Sunny mornings bring forth a
time of Joy
Little children toying with grown up
Ideal to uplift their minds
deep down inside everyone can hold on
to everything that once belong
there are two cornerstones in life
one is to live your life to its
fullest take control of your emotion
Allow nothing but happiness to
enter into your being
two is the sadness that has place
in your life mind and body sadness
can make you forget everything
that were beautiful
loneliness, hurt and pain the right
think for yourself
uplift uplift lift your head up

Life Is a Test

As I walk through this world of
so much hurt and pain
I wonder must there be so much
hurt and pain
suffering is an everyday event
As I look to my left, I see a child
crying for help
I look to right, I see a woman
crying out for help a crack
cocaine habit
As I look behind me I see a
world that is falling apart
the world is a big stage and
everyone is playing part
and I need an Oscar for righteousness For I am accepting on
behalf of Jesus Christ

Summer Love

Summer is about to spring forth
Air is changing
sweet smell of flower blooming
Loneliness become Joy for your
heart pumping for Love
A smile, a rare glow says all
Holding hands walking in the Park
a kiss that make the heart skip
a beat
sneak preview of love at its best
summer love Summer love
emotion a soft voice
saying I love you
Summer love, summer love

Back into Time

My first drag was a blast
my second drag was a trip
that sent my mind back into time
I could see slaves with chains?
of their arms and shackle on their legs
I could see the master with a
whip in his hands and a sadist
Smile on his face
I could see the black women giving
into the master as a way of survival
I could see Nat Turner making a
Successful revolt
I could see Frederick Douglass
Abolishing Slavery
I could see Martin Luther King
saying free at last
I could see all Blacks united as one
shouting Thank God almighty
free at Last Free at Last

Going Home

Going Home I have not been
there in a long time
I can see all my friends and
family before I get there
Going home going home
Someone asks me on trip
where is Home
Mobile, Alabama
Mobile, Alabama
Deep in the south
where the most beautiful
women live
It's going to be a reunion
my mother cooking
my father on the grill
family dancing and showing
Love
Going home, Going home

Love Don't Live Here

We used to stare into each other's eyes
our body would feel the desire
words did not have to be spoken
our hands touch a fire is started
that is the love of the past
our eyes come into contact
there is so much hurt and pain
we have to use words
to keep from destroying each other
we know it's all gone
Some reason we still cling to each other
Let's stop this foolish
Love don't live here
Just empty stares into space
we play a game of lover
when we know love is nonexistent
going through the motion
trying to hold to anything
we have to let it go
Love don't live here
hard as we try
Love don't live here anymore

Loving You

Loving you have been one of the
most beautiful spin the heart feel
everyday thought of being in your presence
the sight of pleasure that you
wake in the mind and body
To hold, caress, burning emotion
Loving you
Daylight, Laugh, Cheer, Joy and Fulfillment
two minds on a flight of enjoyment
and a night to remember
thought Ideal, desire that has
came to place
Let's not be fool
true Love will always stand
strong!!!
A one-way door to happiness
Loving you, Loving you has
has been great for the
heart!!!

Dream of Love

I dream of Love
that will lift my spirit
I dream of Love
that will take my heart
to a level of enchantment
I dream of Love
that will fill my every desire
I dream of Love
that will make me smile on sight
I dream of Love
that will make me smile on sight
I dream of Love
that will turn my sorrow into
Joy!!!
I dream of Love
that will be sweet and gentle
I dream of Love
that will open the heart
to unlimited moment of pleasure
I dream of Love
until the end of time

Tonight the Night

Tonight is the night
there's no doubt this Love of ours
eye contact across the room
a sneak glance, minds working overtime
Tonight is the night
a moment we will learn to cherish forever
lost treasure we both unlock
a thought made one moment notice
two spellbound body waiting for
each other to make a move
Love on the spot, the beginning of
a beautiful moment to come
Tonight the night
a moment we will cherish
and find the crown pleasure of them
tonight the night of many more
a moment we will cherish
tonight the night

Summer in the Air

Summer is in the air,
flowers are blooming
birds singing
children playing in the street
a beautiful sight to behold
everyone traveling to feel enjoyment
no pain or suffering
a moment of nothing but peace
A moment to reach for Love
flashback of a Lost Love
sending you searching into the
wrong direction
good memory fills the mind
a heart with Joy
sad member causes the heart
to reflect on pain and gain
Summer in the air
flowers are blooming
oh, what a year of summer
to fulfill the mind and heart
summer in the Air
Summer in the Air

A Fire Is Burning Inside

Girl you left me lost in a world
where so many need to be found
I'm standing in space hoping you return
Day by day it seems you may not show
I can't stop waiting
you left a fire burning inside 2x
that no one can handle
every hour I experiment with a fire lady
to see if I can lose this burning sensation
only you can control this feeling I have within
A fire is burning inside 2x
begging for your sweet loving
when we make love you are in a class alone
Nothing can compare to your tender hand
caressing my body
The union of two bodies coming together
in sexual pleasure
Girl you left
A fire burning inside 2x
begging for your tender Loving care

I Knew We Have Something Special

We first met we never knew it would
amount to anything
We stay in contact telephone
conversation brought us closer t
he first night together
oh, what beautiful memory
when we said I do
I knew we had something special
we are like any couple misunderstanding may tangle our web
We always talk first
I knew we had something special
God put us together for a reason
our love for each other is strong
that's why I knew we have something special
a love that would last a lifetime
We're share some tears together
our love is a pillow of tenderness
I knew we have something special

Keep Smiling

When love has turned its back
all your friends has betrayed you
don't think of hurting anyone don't
think violence is the answer
keep smiling
Jesus is on your side
give thanks to Lord
Jesus will help you overcome
all your trial and tribulation
Keep smiling
Just keep smiling
ask Jesus to help you
it might not be at the time you
need it it might take a little longer
remember you didn't ask Jesus
help before
He might not be there at that
precise moment
he come sooner than you think
believe in Jesus
keep smiling
keep smiling

Bye, Bye, Baby

I can remember the day we met
on each other's body our eyes were set
That's when I know you would be mine,
we took a chance and found romance,
before I knew it, you were untrue
with another girl you made me blue
But I won't be your fool no no no
I'm leaving right now
Bye, bye, baby
Bye, bye, baby
Bye, bye, Love
Bye, bye, Love
You called me on the phone tell me
you're all alone, saying you want
me back Before you did it you should
have thought of that
Why you have to go and play those games
Only lead to hurt and pain
why you have to go play around,
making me feel like the fool of town
It's gonna stop right here for sure
I'm walking right out the door
I ain't looking back: ain't looking back

No, no, no, no, no
Bye, bye, baby
Bye, bye, baby
Bye, bye, Love
Bye, bye, boy

Written by Toranita LaShe McClain
December 25, 1990

Last Love

Looking back over the time
I had my mistake
long-suffering, pain, and hurt
love have been good and bad
so I am looking
Last Love, Last Love
a love that will stand the test
of time
A love that will endure
the complete packages
A love that the Lord has
put together
Last Love, Last Love
a love that can't be divided
a love that worship together
a love that pray together
a love that is uplifted
that standing on Christian Love
unchanged love, a smile, a kiss
as a show of love
To embrace, a good night kiss
Lord continue to bless this
Love

Blind but Can See

I am fighting with myself
to see all the beauty of world
confused by people
but not blinded by knowledge
I can see with my heart
ever since I have lost my sight
Blind: But can see
I feel everyone that's around me
With a touch, I can see
more than most people
with vision
A shame from hearing
a world that is lost
because of sight
I am glad that I see with
my touch and hearing
A world that is designed to die
Blind: But can see
stand, fall down, cry for help
you are dying with sight
I am living with touch and hearing
Blind: But can see

Mother Love

The beauty of Life is Love
nothing takes the place of Love
first time you heard the word
Love Your mother saying
I love baby
Next come love in a variety
of meaning
Girlfriend then wife
that bring forth Joy Love
Pain and hurt
thing so wrong
the first Love remember
mother Love
doors are open
mother feeds you when you're
hungry
mother Love gives you strength
when you're weak
a mother Love

Lost in Thought

I dream all day and night
thinking of the first time
that we might be together
knowing that we have someone
else
when we see each other
only a house away
neighbor bound by Love
caught in a situation
eye contact lost in thought
see each other
feeling the hurt and pain
ideal of loving each other
not wanting to hurt the ones
we belong to
Lost in thought

I Hope

I hope that the world
could be triangle of Love
loving each other a brother
sister and friend
The world is run by human
not understanding it Lord rule
everything unto Christ
shall stand forever
worldly life is what divide destroy
killing the promise made
through Christ love joy and happiness
Live accordingly to his word
I pray that could look outside
then see the world that
God create for all of us
I hope

Broken Heart

I let Love break my heart
thinking I knew everything
about love
not understand the compass of love
Love cometh south East, west of north
The reaction is the same
loving her so much so much
my vision was destroyed by my heart
Trusting love not my sight
she was my queen
I her king untold truth
someone taking up time
how can love reinvent your mind
generating a state of loneliness
sadness with tears
crying ground of a broken heart

My First Love

Walking into memory
I had a flashback of youth
thinking about my first love
the talk of what to come
making plan for the future
enjoying each other present
thing of marriage
white house picket fence
life being about change
not understanding love
is not always a keeper
something is missing
hoping to fill that empty space
stop sign flashback
a time to rewrite
a time to reunite
my first love

Night without Love

I lay here in bed thinking
about a Romantic holding on
for something we can't have
selfishness illusion and ideal for love
not realize I had the love anyone could have
listen to feeling that I allow
to control my mind and body
listen to my desire knowing that
love is gone
on a roller coaster or downfall
living moment in fake emotion
I call on the love sadness
to give me praise
a night without love

My Baby

You gave me insight
my mind build on emotion
realizing the confusion
you say you are my baby
loving you has been the
greatest
never know what love mean
holding you in my arm has
been a life changing experience
you have opened my eyes and
body to great height
I love you as a summer breeze
Hope that I could fulfil
my mind waiting to say you are
my baby

I Am Yours

I came into the night
bring me into the morning
knowing my love is gone
forever
I can't change a moment
wishing I could bring you
back into my life
change may come only your
love can take me to the next
level
I have felt hurt and pain
never a love to stand forever
removing pitfalls
that can interfere
with our love
I am yours

Sunlight

Sunlight beaming in my room
like a breath of fresh air
realizing there is a virus
taking over the world
death taking on the stage
of the world
a states on a downfall
can't hide or run
facing a life and death
wondering while this is
happy to us
praying the Sunlight will
shine
you pray for those who
gone and pray for those
who standing
No power to change anything
I must call on the main
who have all the power
Jesus, Jesus

Pain

Hello Love can we get together
love swept you off your feet
you cry for days wondering
why is their distrust and
suffering
you think you are the only one
that know friend feeling your hurt
moment of the time spent
together
beautiful flower sent
night of Dancing, walking on
the beach love everywhere
why can you say we are finished
I save my whole life
Never question anything
I really don't know you
what is your name
they call me pain

Clarence McClain Jr.
Born: Mobile, Alabama
Married: Sharon McClain
Kids: Linda, Clarence, Noah, Dion
Step Kids: Chico, Tiawanda, Nina, Zachary
Siblings: Lottie, Olevia, Lois, Henry
Parent: Clarence McClain Sr., Mattie Roberson
Loving Memory: Clarence McClain Sr.

Clarence McClain Jr.
Born: Mobile, Alabama
Married: Sharon McClain
Kids: Linda, Clarence, Noah, Dion
Step Kids: Chico, Tiawanda, Nina, Zachary
Siblings: Lottie, Olevia, Lois, Henry
Parent: Clarence McClain Sr., Mattie Roberson
Loving Memory: Clarence McClain Sr. Mattie
McClain, Lois Dotch, Henry McClain,
Toranita McClain, Michael McClain